Nena No More

By:
Monica Crum

Elite Publishing House
2024

ELITE PUBLISHING
HOUSE
YOUR LEGACY. YOUR BOOK.

First Edition

Copyright 2024 © Monica Crum

All Rights Reserved

No part of this book may be reproduced or transmitted in any form or by any means, electronical or mechanical, including photocopying, recording or by an information storage and retrieval system – except by a reviewer who may quote brief passages in a review to be printed in a magazine, newspaper or on the Web – without permission in writing from the publisher.

Cover Graphics: Kathryn Denhof

To my brother that I couldn't save, and to my family that saved me.
♥

Content Guidance:

This book explores aspects of psychology and mental health and contains depictions of self-harm, abuse, and suicide. Please read with care.

The National Suicide Prevention Lifeline is a hotline for individuals in crisis or for those looking to help someone else. To speak with a certified listener, call 1-800-273-8255.
Crisis Text Line is a texting service for emotional crisis support. To speak with a trained listener, text HELLO to 741741. It is free, available 24/7, and confidential.

TABLE OF CONTENTS

PREFACE *10*

COLLECTION OF POEMS *16*

A NOTE ABOUT MY FAMILY *118*

EDDIE'S INTRODUCTION *121*

EPILOGUE... *123*

ACKNOWLEDGEMENTS *125*

ABOUT THE AUTHOR *127*

Preface

They call me Nena...

My father gave me this nickname. In Spanish, it means little girl. Though I should consider it an affectionate appellation, it represents a moniker of pain. Sometimes I look back on my life and wonder how I survived.

My twin brother Eddie and I were born in San Antonio, Texas, in 1973. Our parents only stayed married for a short time. My mother said that my father was abusive to her during her pregnancy, so shortly a year after we were born, they split up. My brother and I were in a foster home until their divorce was final, and then, our father was given custody.

My mother remarried and had three more children with my stepdad. My father remarried when my brother and I turned four, and from that moment forward, things were different.

Life started to change when I was six years old. For starters, when we started school, my brother changed. He let the kids at school influence him, and he misbehaved in class. Also, kids bullied him. My brother and I grew up poor, and we also were biracial. It wasn't easy being half Hispanic/ half white. My father's family came from Mexico, and my mother's family is Irish American, so growing up in the predominantly Hispanic side of town was difficult. My brother and I were called racial slurs like honky, white-ass, whetto, which means "light skin boy," and whetta, which means "light skin girl," and so on. Kids were mean, and we were not accepted like others were. We were judged by class and color.

In addition, my father's abuse started when we were about six years old. At first, it was just spankings, and then he started taking things away from us. Eventually, his actions progressed to torture and mind games, which progressively got worse. The abuse/torture was intense. He broke my collarbones—both of them. Our father beat us often, whipping us with homemade paddles from work, cedar 2x4s. He'd make us kneel in corners all day by the fireplace. Sometimes, he locked up the fridge so we couldn't eat. His controlling of the household food progressed to the extent that he counted the cookies in the cookie jar, and if the number wasn't equal to some magical digit in his head, then we got beat. My brother frequently tried to escape by sneaking out of the house or running away, and as such, he was often handcuffed to the bed at night.

Sometimes it's all a blur, but I distinctly remember my first abusive episode from a time when I was probably around six. I was crying from being disciplined, and my father screamed at me to stop. Because I wouldn't quit crying, my father shoved my face under a cold running faucet in the bathtub until I stopped crying. Of course, I stopped because I couldn't breathe.

I was around seven years old the first time my father slapped me, punched me in my face, spanked me, then picked me up and threw me up against a built-in dresser in the wall. The dresser handles hit my spine, and I've never been the same since.

Our lives centered on simple moments between constant beatings and spankings—torture. And when one of us was being beaten, my stepmom would hold my brother or me so we could not come in and rescue each other. We both felt so helpless— being restrained, hearing screaming and crying on the other side of the door.

We weren't allowed to join clubs, extracurricular activities, GT classes at school, or honors classes. We were not allowed to do anything that cost him time or money. But we *did* have to work. Starting in first grade, we threw newspaper routes for my dad seven days a week. We also collected payments on Friday nights and Saturday mornings.

Ultimately, we had no time for childhood. Very rarely did we play. At a moment's notice, we were at his beck and call.

My brother and my grandmother kept me afloat. Then, after I turned twelve years old, my grandmother died. Five months later, my brother moved in with our mother, leaving me alone with our father and stepmother.

I was alone, with no one to talk to—to protect me. I became suicidal and depressed. I didn't know it yet, but I was bipolar.

I later discovered that my brother also suffered from Bipolar depression and ADHD. In addition, he was a paranoid schizophrenic who often suffered from suicidal thoughts. He wanted my father's affection and approval. He never got it.

I, myself, suffer from PTSD, Bipolar depression, and suicidality. So, sometimes, I don't see things the way they truly are or how other people see them. And obviously, I have trust issues because of my father.

My mental disorder only added to the torture of the physical, mental, emotional, and verbal abuse I endured.

My father told me every day that we should have never been born. And I believed him. So did my brother.

My brother did time in prison and became homeless. He suffered from drug abuse, making it difficult to hold a job. He was also very violent. Many times, I had to detach myself from him. After many periods where he came in and out of my life, he eventually stopped checking up on me at all.

Life without my brother was hard to deal with. After all, the abuse made us co-dependent. I loved him so much, and because we were twins, I felt a part of me had died.

Then on July 23rd, 2021, I got a phone call and learned that my twin brother had died in Los Angeles, California, from an overdose of fentanyl. He died in a bathroom stall in a homeless shelter. He died alone, and I wasn't there to protect him.

Needless to say, my life hasn't been easy. I thank God every day that he helped me through it all. Although, every day is a battle. God continues to help me, even now. It's the real reason I get up every day. I am blessed and grateful to have a husband and children who are patient and understanding.

I love my husband and my children very much. I don't want to hurt them or disappoint God, so instead of taking my own life, I have endured.

Mental illness affects many people today, yet we have been told our whole lives not to talk about it. The world is changing, though, and society, in general, has become more aware of mental illness and ways to work through it.

Through my struggles, I've learned that you can't go on in without acknowledging your feelings. Emotions are the driving force behind everything we do in life.

You are important. We all are. Taking care of your mental state is also important.

Don't let anyone make you believe any different. You are not to blame for any abuse you may have encountered or are going through.

My writings are dark because some places in my mind will always be dark, but some are bright. I've allowed to let the sun shine through my broken pieces. When I write about sadness or hurting myself, I emancipate my iniquity. Once it's on paper, I release that burden—those awful feelings. Then, I feel better. When it's down on paper, it's out of my mind.

Writing is my therapy, though I still see a therapist, and I'm working on myself daily.

If you're reading this book, I hope you learn something from my words. If you accept one mantra from my words, I hope it is this: "This too shall pass."

You *can* overcome your circumstances. You are beautiful and unique. There is only one of you. You cannot be replaced. So, take care of your precious self.

I hope you like my book.

Collection of Poems

The End

The end of my childhood
Was marked by the disappointment
Of my life.
 There I was, sitting in the tub
Crying over my wounds and my wounded heart.
My cuts bleeding into the water,
At only the age of 6.
My broken bones were never set.
Pleading for mercy from God,
 to take away the pain in my heart.
I could handle the inflicted wounds
Of my father,
But my heart suffered so much more.
The beating in my chest started to
Change,
For a rage was burning.

Once

I was poetry once, you see
Life was new, and I would sing
Of birds and rainbows and the sky of blue
And how every day was always new

I was poetry once, you see
I used to believe in magic
I used to believe in you and me
And now, it seems, life is so tragic

I was poetry once, you see
Now, I am a wasted song
Where children cry, there is no we
And everything feels so wrong

Bad Times

Looking into the corners of my mind,
I start to remember bad times gone dormant
Reaching through the darkness and pain
Trying to push out all the sadness
Reflecting on the scolding,
The tears, and the chill in the air
It was hard to breathe
To live and to grow.
Dark rooms, holes in the floor,
And crickets in the background, playing songs of sadness
Torn walls and days gone bad
I want to disappear and die

This was not a home,
and it was all wrong in every way
Wanting to throw away these memories
But not even time wants them
 They have crept into every part of my mind, my soul.
Refusing to leave, remaining forever.

Reflections

Reflections of the past
    Times of innocence
        Turned to Tragedy
    Times of playful laughter
        Turned to Cries for help

Reflections of the past
    Play inside my head now
    Like a broken record that can't be fixed
    Like a scratch along the vinyl of life
    Can't be repaired, only stuck to repeat
        Over and over and over

The white noise of cries and screams
    Play in the background
    As his whip lashes us
        Over and over and over

The tears are soft and wet, flowing over my cheeks
As I wait for 2:30 to come again
    Every day
        Forever

The Struggle

I **g a s p** for air

∞

I **s t r u g g l e** to breathe
He's too **s t r o n g**.
He won't let go

∞

The water **r u s h e s** over my head.
It's so **C O L D**.

∞

The water **f l u s h e s**
Into my eyes, into my nostrils, into my mouth

∞

I **t w i s t** and **k i c k**
He holds my hair tight

∞

I move my head and try to
S C R E A M,
But he puts me back under

∞

I hear him say to stop crying, but it
H U R T S.

∞

He hits my bottom, and I c r y harder

I'm **TERRIFIED**.

No one comes to help me

∞

I stop crying…

I hope to **DIE** soon

So he'll let go…

∞

A n d t h e n, h e l e t s g o.

Not enough

Not enough experience in life for the marriage of two people
That were never meant to be.
Their love was meaningless,
And so, it gave birth to meaningless children.
There was not enough love to keep the family together,
So, they said their goodbyes and parted ways.
The boy was not enough to bring pride to his father's heart...
The girl was not bright enough to make her father shine.
And so, it began the journey of never being enough...
For anyone—or anything.

Grandma

My grandma was beautiful in every single way
She would sit at her window sometimes just to see me play
She would tell me how pretty I was
And take me to the store
It was so fun to be with her
It was her I adored
She would debone my fish before I put it in my mouth
She would sing to me after my dad would chew me out
My grandma would brush and curl my hair at night
And she would give me hugs and hold me oh so tight
"Dame besitos" she would say to me, sweet
And my brother and I would kiss her on each side of her cheek
She smelled like perfume and loved to wear gold
To me, she was strong, amazing, and bold
I miss my grandma's voice and her beautiful face
But most of all, I miss her sweet, warm embrace.

Mother

Dreaming of my mother makes me oh-so sad
Dreaming of her holding me makes me oh-so mad
I wish she would just tell me it's going to be alright
That she would be there taking care of me, all through the night
Dreaming of her braiding my hair and calling me dear,
She would say words of wisdom softly in my ear
I wish she could give me kisses, sweet and oh-so kind
And I would be her child until the end of time
Wake me from this dream, for none of this is real
My heart is broken into pieces, and now I cannot feel.

Twins, We Will Always Be

You were there from day one
Like the morning sun
To brighten up my day
With your smile while we played.
We walked through woods together
And swam with one another.
You would catch the light bugs, and I would set them free.
You and I were half of each other
Twins, we will always be...
I remember playing football with you until the sun went down.
We always had some watermelon as a treat to cool us down.
We used to sing about God and how he would heal our pain,
But now I sit with all my tears that forever fall like rain.
One day, I will see you again and make new memories
Because you see, as I said before,
Twins, we will always be.

A Million Tears

I could cry a million tears
 for a million years,
and still not empty all the sadness
in my soul.

Autumn

Autumn came early the year you died
The leaves started falling, and I could do nothing but cry
Your passing was so sudden, and
oddly unexpected was the feeling
 of being lonely,
for once in my whole life.

You left behind a legacy
Not one of nobility
But one of estrangement from a family
You once knew, you once hated
Yet you knew you were all I had

I was the only one who mourned for you
You leave behind me, your sister
Your twin, your half of you.

I will cry in silence, for no one knows
the pain I have endured
For you were the only one who knew
 the pain we shared together.

For autumn came early the year you died
And the leaves will fall forever,

And so will My tears.

PTSD

PTSD...
Call it what you will.
My heart is pounding
And everything is still.
My hands are getting sweaty.
My stomach starts to hurt.
The room is feeling heavy
And so does my shirt.

I want to run and hide.
I want to feel safe.
No one is by my side.
No one ever came.
My body starts to shake.
My feelings start to crumble.
My body starts to quake.
I hope I won't stumble.

I enter down this path
Of complete and lonely terror.
I can feel his wrath.
I can feel the horror.
I can hear the screaming.
I can taste the blood.
I am not dreaming.
 He will be judged.

I live with these memories
That I constantly fight.
They come for me steadily,
Even at night.

Don't!

Don't begin to tell me you cared for him so,
Don't tell me that you mourned for him.
Don't Tell Me Anymore.

Don't tell me his death made your heart break in two
Don't tell me you can't go on.
Just tell me the truth.

Tell me you're relieved and couldn't wait to smile.
With his death that came so sudden, there is no denial.
You were happy for my loss; you couldn't wait to tell.
You were lost in your thoughts, while I was in my hell.
You can go on now—go about your day
While I still mourn and lose myself in dismay.

The Gathering

Ladies, gather beside me
And cry tears of sadness with me.
I have been entranced by my failers
And have been stirred
By my thoughts of self-harm.
I am sleeping in the longest,
Darkest night that has ever been.
Please stay and weep with me,
For tomorrow, with hope,
I may awake.

Eternally Damned

Pay no attention to the woman crying in the corner.
She weeps over her transgressions.
She was stupid and foolish to think
That none would care if she hated herself and the people in her world.
She paid no mind to the people who cared for her, so she hurt them in every way.
She thought only of herself, and now she is lost in her tears—
Tears that no one will shed for her anymore.
She is eternally damned within herself to hear all the voices in her head
Telling her she was wrong and that she should have known better.
These voices get louder every day.
They make sure she never gets any rest
Let her guilt and pain eat her up inside until she is no more,
For it is a better death for her than anyone could give her.
Let her rot in her own misery and regret.
She will pay for all the tears she shed over her stupidity,
For no one will remember her in the end—
Or care to call her name.

Lifeless

Take my heart, if you will
My breath is shallow
And my heart is still
No feelings left inside
My blood has drained out
My heart has stopped beating
It waits for its disposal.

Not Dreaming

Does it please you to kill me in your dreams?
Do you hold my neck in your hands with excitement?
Or after you have strangled the life out of me,
Do you wake up to see me breathing and think,
"How wonderful. I've committed no crime."

Do you seek justice in your dreams because there is none for you awake?
In your dreams, are you peeling the skin from my flesh and hearing my screams?
Do you smile?
And when you wake to see me in one piece and think,
"How wonderful. I've committed no crime."

Does your gun touch my head and go off into my skull
When it shatters it into a million pieces
Do you think,
"Now we're even."

But you're not dreaming yet...

Release

To feel the blade against my skin
To feel release all over again
I taste my tears falling down my cheeks
I feel so vulnerable and so weak

My thoughts of all the pain I feel
Will soon be over when I touch steel
My blood will pour out on my skin
And I will feel release again.

Please Just Red and Black

I only see in black and red—
The blackness of shadows that loom over the darkness of my heart
And red for the pain and grief and blood that I have felt—and that I have lost.
There is no yellow sunshine or any blue sky, maybe grey for the clouds
Filled with my tears of sadness over the love I have lost—and the pain I have felt.
No green grass or pink and orange horizons.
No beautiful mornings or new days of hope.
Just red and black.
My bloody red heart is full of blackness.
It has a hole that cannot be filled with anything but pain...
And...
Heartache.

Let Me Sleep

Death, do not wake me up.
Meet me in my dreams,
And take me to endless nights of solitude.
Take me to where I can't hear music and laughter.
I don't want to see the sun
And all the pain it brings to my soul.
Yet let me sleep in death
Where there is peace and quiet
Where there are no more thoughts, no more guilt…
No more me.
Oh, how I hate living in this awful world of uncertainty—
And pain.
Regret follows me and watches me around every corner,
Waiting to catch me.
But I run fast onto the darkness.
Until I'm home, asleep.
Waiting to be taken by you.
Death, be my savior,
And kiss me on my cheek before you take me.
Agree to take me sleeping
So that I may die with a sweet dream in my heart…
So that I may sin no more.
I long to see you,
Like a child missing her mother.
I do hope you come for me soon

To rescue me from this torment in my heart
To save me from myself and all the awful things I have inflicted on others.
Take me now.
I'm ready!

The Moment

Breathing heavy
Looking at my skin and
Anticipating what I'm going to do
Wishing I had done it sooner

Holding the knife
I'm entranced by the sharpness
Of its cold, silver, shiny blade
Hoping it will release me

Pressing it down on my skin
I gasp for air and hold my breath
My blood pours out
And once again
I am free.

;

I chose to continue a story that started out with disaster.
My story is full of broken hearts,
Broken dreams,
Broken promises.
Was it too much to ask for a normal life with normal parents?
What is normal?
These days, normal is going a hundred—from nine to five
While the world around you asks the impossible
As you try to function from growing up in a dysfunctional home.

I chose to continue my story,
Even though the happily ever after may be too far down the road.
My purpose is to finish what I started.
But it hurts…
It stabs me.
At times, the pain blinds me
As my heart begs me to put it out of its misery.
Disappointment is constant.
With no end in sight.
I am disillusioned by hope.
I do my best, staying positive,
yet the reality is surreal.

Can you?

Can I tell you my mind is starting to break?
Can I tell you that my heart is splitting in to pieces?
Can I tell you all my pain ,as you go through yours?
Can you handle my plight, and carry it too?
Can you understand my battle and make a treaty for me?
Can you hold me in your arms and not know why?
Can you stay beside me until the end?

I Am Sadness

I am sadness...
I dwell on the pain I've encountered
And the pain I've inflicted.
I see the troubled past and think
Of ways I could have changed it.

I don't care about the present,
For sadness can only dwell,
In the past, where it cannot change.
But it grows and it feeds on reminiscence.
On times gone and never to be again.

I live on sadness and cafe lattes.
On lost dreams and what-could-have beens.
So, leave me be and let me ponder
Over my tears and my letdowns,
And everything in between.

Peace

I crawl into bed every night
Hoping to find a dream to help me through my plight.

My body aches, and I'm full of thoughts that play over and over.
They just won't stop.

I pray that my sins will be forgiven and I'll make it through the night.
But my fears and worries overwhelm me.
They are so hard to fight.

I hope to find peace one day since I have none.
Maybe in my sleep, I'll find something beautiful, something small.

Since peace is small and fragile and something you can hold,
I will hold it next to me
Even when I'm cold.

I'm going to close my eyes now and hold onto my bed
In hopes that I find peace through all this gloom and dread.

Blanket

Death is like a blanket
That covers me in the night.
It keeps me warm with the comfort of knowing
That it will end all of my sorrows at the end of the day.
For nothing is more permanent, more concrete, more certain
Than the ending of my life.

Corners

Alone with my thoughts, I ponder with dread
About all the darkness inside my head
Some corners are black and cold
Some things are forgotten because I'm getting old.
Other places are alive and constantly fighting
To take over my mind, and so I keep writing
Hoping, one day, to feel somewhat alive
And start to live, to dream, to thrive.

Regret

I wish I could make you unsee all the things you've seen,
Unhear all the things you have heard,
Unfeel all the things that hurt you.
Then, and only then, you would be free,
To see all the amazing things around you,
To hear all the beautiful sounds and
To feel all the wonderful things.
How I wish to find that beautiful star
And wish on it and see what it could do!
I would leave this Earth on my last breath
Knowing I would never live again
To find that star for you.
I would wish upon it knowing
That you would be happy and free
And would live again.

What I'm Supposed to Be

I was supposed to be the twinkle in your eye,
But your eyes were too blind to see that,
I was supposed to be the joy in your heart,
But your heart was too dead to know,
That I was supposed to be your sunshine.
Instead, I was the dark cloud around you.
I was supposed to be your reason to live.
Instead, I was your reason to die.
I was supposed to be a gift for you.
Instead, you wished you could give me back.

You hurt me—
You beat me—
You broke my bones—
You told me I should have never been born.
I was supposed to be a happy little girl,
Now I'm only an empty shell...
Guess that's what I was supposed to be all along.

The Cloud

My day becomes endless,
With nonsense and confusion.
I try to make sense of things,
Only to return to my cloud of uncertainty.
Things upside down seem right,
And I smile with delight.
And then reality sets in, with horror.
And I'm lost in doubt—no end in sight.
My hands on my face, hiding my eyes,
While the procrastination of my life's ending sweeps through my thoughts.
Will sanity itself return?
Can things be real again?
I wait in silence...

They

My thoughts start quiet and small
Not knowing how they will grow
I have to keep them to myself
Since sometimes I can't explain them

They can choke me
They can anger me
They can fill me with fear

They come from within
They haunt my dreams
They scream at me
They threaten my life

Before I know it, I am
Paralyzed by confusion
Trying to make sense of
All of the nonsense inside me.

Silence

I just want the whole world to be quiet for five minutes!

Death

Death can be so final—
So black, so cold.
It can be so climactic
So loud, so bold.
Death doesn't need a reason
To come in and destroy.
It just does what it wants.
Death feeds on the innocent.
It feeds on the good and the bad,
The happy and the sad.
It prays on the strong and the weak.
It keeps me humble and meek.

I Just Want…

I just want to end it all and slam into a wall.
Just let it be said that Monica is dead.
I'm screaming and crying and I feel like I'm dying.
Why can't anyone hear me ,or see me, or feel me?
I'm a complete mess, I'm in distress!
Just want to cry, just want to die.
I mess everything up. I'm a screw up.
Needing to bleed ,I've planted my seed.
Can't wait to not exist ,oh what sweet Bliss!
I'm on the verge, I feel the urge
I'm sitting still and I feel ill.
My stomach rumbles but I'm ready to crumble
My head hurts bad deep within I am sad
Feeling suicidal I sit here and idle.

Melancholy

Maybe it's the weather.
Maybe I'm a bit melancholy because of it.
Maybe it's for no reason—or too many reasons to speak of.
My mind drifts to the silence in the room.
I hear the birds outside the window
As the June bugs hit the front door glass.
The gloomy, yet well-lit sky outside
Makes it hard to think straight.
Missing so much in my life
And dwelling on what might have—what should have beens.
The TV is on in the background.
Its sounds like muffled words as the branches outside sway back and forth,
And it's almost hypnotic.
I can almost hear the beating of my heart
 And then my eyes tear up from staring too long out the window.
 Seeing my past and future all at once.
My heart feels still now.
I don't know if I'm happy or sad,
But I do know that the wind will stop,
The TV will turn off,
The birds will go to sleep, and the sun will set.
But I will remain as I was before.

Chaos

I feel I'm nothing but a chaotic mess of disappointments
Wishing something would ignite my soul. That something
would bring to life some sort of order and
anticipation of the next day.

Desperation

Why must this journey of life be so hard and arjous.
 Why must everyday be unfulfilling and disappointing?
 I am certain that I will lose all hope someday .
 My heart has been stabbed and forgotten.
 All that is left is a shell of a person who struggles
 to breathe this thick and disgusting air of life.
 It seeks to smother me with its hate and pain.
My past haunts me and wants me to die a horrible death
 along with all the other forgotten souls of the past.
 I struggle every day to walk, to breathe.
Why must I allow happiness to set in when it will be taken away
 from me and thrown into the pit we're all beautiful things go to die?
And yet I still struggle to hold on to my hope that one day
 my God will take all of my sadness and pain
 and crush it into granule pieces and blow it into existence.
To finally rid me of all of my nightmares, my disappointments,
my guilt, and help me feel free again.
 Oh, how I long to be alive and feel alive!
 This life has been a curse for me.
 I'm running into desperation for my life.

Defeated

"Feeling defeated."
That's what they call it
When your heart and mind
Don't know where to go anymore.
When you have exhausted all efforts,
Your last-ditch effort,
Throwing the towel at it all.
Your ace in the hole was a joker
And it laughed at your disappointment.
You saw it all, and you wish you hadn't.
Now, you are left with nothing
But the prize of being defeated.
The willingness to go no further.
Sit and be amazed how the world will go on…
And leave you behind.

Because I Must

I do not face today because I want to,
But Because I must.
I do not breathe today because I want to
But Because I must
I do not plan for tomorrow because I want to
But because I must.
I do not write this poem because I want to
But Because I must.

Mask

My mask is pleasant and common
Only those that are observant
Can see through it
You must get past the smile
The careful side of me,
To get past the laughter and giggles
I have learned to wear it well
I am composed and patient.
Yet behind my eyes,
I am breaking down and screaming!
I'm catching my breath
So, I don't die from humiliation
People look at me strangely
Knowing something is different
So, I look away and turn back with a smile
It's what's acceptable
It's what's expected.
Can't break down in the middle of the store, or the bank, or the freeway.
But I want to.

For You

Your body is like a broken poetry book.
Full of pain and unspoken sadness.
Lost pages of small moments of happiness.
Torn and wasted pages of broken pieces
That your heart felt and has left behind.
You want out, and to burn your life to ashes.
But your obligations keeps you here.
Know that when your poetic life ends
Your book will be burned and only
The pages of happiness will remain.

Lost

Lost and confused are my days.
While I sift through my past,
Trying to conquer
What I do not understand.

Failing

A complete mess is what I am every day.
Trying to cling on to every morsel of hope.
I am feeling low and as my spirit is slowly dying.
I feel the need to keep trying harder.
To look for my reasons to survive.
But I am failing, tragically.

Tortured

The pain I have inside is crippling.
 It twists and bends me into ways that I cannot function.
 I'm tortured by thoughts that I cannot send away,
And my dreams are screams of the past wanting to be released.

Trapped

Why can't I fly?
Have I not a sweet voice to sing with
And arms to lift me?
With sleep filled eyes
I lay softly on my pillow to dream ,
Of wings that will grant me flight
To the ends of the earth.
Like a bird with granted wishes
Of endless nights soaring above the clouds,
Yet under the stars.
Caught between two worlds am I.
Wanting to fly far away,
 But trapped in a cage of despair.

Contempt

I have contempt for the state of my soul.
I live in-between the fabrics of time stitched together
 by memories that make no sense to me and others that haunt
me.
The memories are revolving on a constant loop of thought.
I rip apart my feelings, trying to find some content, some sense of
where I'm at,
But so much confusion exists in my mind.
Torn in the here and now, and the past , is an arduous journey for
me to walk through.
Pretending to be content with life, and struggling with my dissat-
isfaction of it all at once.

Condemnation

There is no safety in my lonely moments
The ringing in my ears
The beating of my heart
Listening to it shatter into a thousand pieces
My mind is scrambling for comprehension
Confused of why my misery haunts me
It won't leave and it tears me to my core
Suffering in solitude is my condemnation
I have no peace for my sins
No peace for my heartache.
I stand here and watch my heart gather
What's left over
Starving for life,
for acceptance,
for redemption.

Stuck

I'm so confused
In a constant state of **stuck**
Not being able to see my own potential
Stuck in a grind
Lost in my thoughts,
In my worries and my state of being

Why can't I get this?
Why can't I just get this right?
I want to see me see straight
To see me for all I'm worth
To soar high above my faults,
And sense of doubt
To be one with my inner self,
To be complete.

The Storm

The clouds are dark and grey
They are filled with the songs of my sadness
The rains starts to fall
And the raindrops sing to me
Drip, drop, drip, drop
It's starts slow… and then begins the deluge
The pounding of thunder is in rhythm with the beats of my heart
The storm is over me as tears burst out of my eyes.
The Cracking of thunder echoes as my heart breaks in two
The symphony of music plays on the roof as I cry and expel all the pain inside
As my tears slow down, the rain starts to move away.
The storm has brought down tears of lessons learned
And has watered seeds of hope
As I lay down to rest,
The thunder sings me to sleep
AND the storm follows another broken heart.

Sadness

Sliding into sadness every single night
pulling myself back up is such an awful plight
Thinking of all my sadness in every single day
Haunts every thought in every single way.
I know it seems so daunting and extremely so obscure
To ever think of happiness when life is full of curves
To Always be uncertain of what truly lies ahead
Forever filled with solace, that my heart is completely dead
Knowing I don't matter, that my existence is left of right
Knowing that my sadness is mine through all my life.

Untitled

My heart is bleeding out and there is no way to clean it up.

Unheard

Lost in a world of millions
Fighting for a voice.
Yet if you listen carefully
You will hear my screams
In the pit of your stomach.

Silence

Your unconscious state of being tells all
Your silence is deafening
As you take your secrets to the grave.
Your body is lifeless, incoherent, and silent
Yet it screams to be avenged
To take back what was taken
To right a wrong
No one knows the moments that played out before your end
But this I do know…
I will speak for you
Even in death, you will not be silenced
Others will hear of you and your story told
And one day, we will meet again.

The Shadows

The sun once again in the window
Casts its sadness over the floor.
The shadows on the wall tell me it's afternoon,
And that sick feeling engulfs me again.
Feelings of terror,
and waiting for a punishment that will never come.
Feeling I've done wrong to no one,
but everyone.
I hide my feeling of fear
by scratching my head,
twisting my hair
and squirming my feet over each other.
I start to breathe fast
then I can't catch my breath.
The TV gets louder,
and I can hear the clock ticking on the wall.
I hear the sound in my ears starting to deafen me.
As I close my eyes and wait for the worst
It all stops,
and I run to throw up.
I wash my face as tears run down.
And the sun starts to set in the window.

Nothingness

Take my hand
 Till the colors run through .
Till they bleed into walls of
Nothingness untrue.

The walls will collapse
And forward goes the door,
Of emptiness and sorrow
Till it shatters on the floor .

Weak are the mumbles of
Unfortunates and sinners.
And cold are the stares
Of the glorious and winners.

Back and Forth

Contemplating the end of one's life is not an easy thing to do.
The constantly going over to be or not to be is truly the real question.
You are constantly reminded of your past in the present.
Life is full of pain and misery and the happy moments are few and far between.
Yet you go on existing because self-preservation goes into play.
 The pain you're going through will end when you die, but it will be transformed into something worse, something hated.
 For those who mourn you will have lost something valuable, and so they will hate you more .
 They will carry your burden of your pain and your death, for your pain will have nowhere to run, but to them. Into the brick wall that is ,everyone you knew.
 So, you fight another day, another dark moment, another day of Russian roulette.
 Will your mind kill you; will the day kill you, or will you bring your pain to its knees as you crush it with all your might to exist?
Your future is still unwritten.

Infiltrating

My sadness stabs me
Piercing through my chest
It starts to multiply as it spreads all over
It hurts me deeply.
I can't breathe at all
Thinking of all the sadness that perplexes my life constantly
Sleepless nights and wounded thoughts
Make for a night filled with dreams of horror and tearful moments
That don't stop and invade every corner of my brain
Wishing it would all go away
Thinking of nothing at all would be a treat
It would give me time to heal
Yet in doesn't relent; it keeps going
Stabbing, digging, infiltrating every day, every moment
Always.

Unappetizing

Some of my thoughts are not for human consumption.
Some are full of pain, and the taste is bitter.
It rolls on my tongue and makes me want to vomit.
Thoughts that are hard to breakdown, and chew.
To swallow thoughts of anger, and rage is unappetizing.
My diet is ruined constantly with thoughts of self-infliction and death.
So, I keep these thoughts safe in the back of the fridge where are leftovers are kept.
They can spoil and fester in the cold parts of my mind.
They smell of disease, and this infects my brain.
With putrid memories of a rotting past
Waiting to be thrown out for disposal.

Existing

Living is exhausting .
My existence is merely
Of convenience for those around me.
The unfortunate thoughts
That go through my mind plague me
With misfortune and misguided feelings.
This life has no prize at the end
But of loneliness and darkness in my
Grave of eternity.
The cloud I'm in is cold and grey.
Set to be part of me ,
I breathe it in and it grows from my sadness
Why do I continue to exist ?
To live, to bleed?

Shadows

Shadows play in the background
And it's movements entrance me
The clouds are covering the sky with darkness.
Will the sun set for my sadness?
Will it mourn for the loss of my mind?
I want to grab the clouds from the sky
and put them under my head as a pillow,
Then cover my body with the blanket of darkness at night.
So that I may dream of all that is dear to me,
Until the madness takes over,
until the sadness takes over,
Pleading for my release,
I struggle to Go on.

Deception

I'm not going to try to
Sift through and try to decipher
The nonsense you brought to my table every day.
I will not try to look into your deception and find truth.
Nor will I try to look for sincerity, where none exists.
Your twisted thoughts,
 and half-truths have made me ill and apprehensive.
Your smile of admiration has given me moments of pause.
Where they smiles of appreciation or smiles of a deeper nature?
Smiles of deception are easy to hide
When no one suspects.
But you are the suspect.
You have lost my friendship
At the crossroads of trust and deceit
Where you decided to take the road to hide your true intentions.
But do not fear, for your true self has shown its dark colors
And in the midst of pain, I will continue as I was before... without you.

Fade

Set my soul on fire
And let me fade away
I have wallowed in misery
And I have endured such pain
Let me go into darkness
And let me be in peace
For I will finally know
That feeling of true release.

Lies

Your tedious lies
And moments of deceit
Are hard to get past, as you sit
In your seat
You tickle my ear
With sayings of truth
But you walk away groaning
As if you were mute.
The real you is hiding
Waiting for release
Hiding behind eyes
That have no peace.

To Know

I wish I didn't know what wrong with me inside.
To know the monstrous plague that has taken over my life
To know that my existence is completely out of my control.
I want to be reborn into a life that is empty of all incoherent thought
To be in knowledge of all that is set out to be lived
To be constant of truth like the blood in my veins
Always flowing, always reliant.

I Pray

I prayed to God for strength
In the middle of the night
I pray to God to comfort me
And help me through this fight
No one knows the pain
Or the sorrow that's inside me
My tears, they fall like rain
But God is there to guide me
One day, my pain will go
And I will smile once again
But for now, God will hold me
Until my sadness ends.

Monologue Inside

The monologue in my mind continues to go on.
 No matter the day, the time.
It starts off small, then ignites the roar of
Places, and people I do not know.
They speak to each other as if I'm not there.
Then they talk to me as if I have the answers.
My intrusive thoughts yell at me.
Thoughts of hurting myself, thoughts of pain, thoughts I do not share.
They do not yield, they are constant
I try to listen to my voice, but they push me
Until I submit and listen.
Circumstances and persuasiveness
Are perpetually rotating inside.
I do not know peace; I cannot think anymore.
Closing my eyes to it all
Closing my mind to rest, until it starts tomorrow.

Emptiness

I beg for death each day to come
And she whispers to me in my ear.
Sweet are the words she repeats
As my neck suddenly gets cold.
 She teases me with laughter
As she passes by me again.
Warm are the thoughts of no thoughts
And comforting are the ideas of emptiness.
My despair would cease
And so would my pain
And all of the unhappiness in between.
Yet she mocks my pain and continues
 to take others to the place my heart knows all to well.
One day though my moment will arrive
It'll be when my heart is warm
Ready to live, ready to be at peace
Yes that day will be glorious indeed.
For that will be the day she snatches my breath
And allows me to sleep forever.

Floating

Warm is the water that covers my body
Yet, as shallow as it is, it still brings warmth like a blanket in the night.
The water makes bubbles as I move in it, slowly turning over.
My hair flowing in the ripples as my calmness takes over me.
As I close my eyes ,music takes me.
It resonates in my mind, all of the perfect moments, never to be repeated again.
My hands feel wrinkled ,and yet I cannot leave this place of unrelenting calmness.
It speaks to my heart and mind, that everything will be alright.
 It will be the way it's supposed to be.
 I can see my toes, small like a child's.
The smell of lavender fills my nose, as I swim away into eternity.

Alone

Written by M.E. 11-28-2018

You open my eyes, that I might find Glory's light around me.
I closed my eyes to the warmth that was pumping in my heart.
You lifted my eyes so that I may greet the future at destiny's Dawn.
I rested my eyes upon the assurance of those dreams.
You opened my eyes to find love on fire.
I closed my eyes to see it was only me.
You gave me eyes to see desire.
I lost my vision to tears never seen.
We had forever to get this life right, and it all started at my site;
Attached to every word, indeed, our lifetime of memories will never leave.
No burden is greater than an image that will not go away—
A constant repetition of patterns etched deep in the brain.
And solitude chases no ghost away.
It only serves to extend the pain.
You open my eyes while I return alone.

Guest

As I feel the rain fall on my face
I'm reminded of the sadness that resides in my heart.
It pulled up a chair, sat down, and decided to feast on my traumas, my letdowns, my
        disappointments, and fears.

I have asked it to leave, yet it has enjoyed the meal too much and wants to stay.
It is like a guest that won't leave. It has overstayed its welcome.

I find ways to get rid of sadness.
I cry it out. I scream it out. I even find moments of happiness to dwell on.
But it knows these are temporary moments, and sadness will slip in and destroy my days, my
        dreams, my moments of accomplishment.

When it finally leaves, I'm left with a broken heart and a loneliness only I truly know well.
For sadness has made its home and will be back soon.

Ready to dine again.

Next time...

Do you see her standing there
With her face all dirty and her stringy hair everywhere
And her hair covering her little shoulders?
Her little dress is tattered and torn on the edge
Her feet are bare and black on the bottom, and her little hands have calluses from hard work.
She's afraid to look up.
As she bows her head, she's afraid to make a sound.
She sits on her bed at night and rocks herself to sleep, wondering why she is alive...
And why her daddy hates her so much.
She prays to God and asks him to take away her pain
She'll do better next time...
And maybe Daddy won't hit her.
As she goes to bed, her body hurts from her broken bones and bruises—
Not remembering why she was hurt.
She'll do better next time...
There's always next time.

Worthlessness

This world is full of hopelessness and gives birth to worthless fruitage
And the worthlessness that comes forth from the earth lives in the streets
And in the homes of those who chose to make all the terrors of life into reality .
I am disgusted by its filth and its murderous ways,
By its deceiving traits and manipulative ideas.
It conjures ways to mislead those of false hope. Getting in the minds of the weak.
The menu offered to all is power, lust, youth, money.
Yet all of these dishes are filled with disgusting ingredients.
It is poison to all who eat from it, and therefore their waste is toxic to the earth.
And so, the cycle continues of worthless produce,
worthless people that have no idea what they have done.

The Antidote

No matter what, you can't cushion the blow,
 to appease yourself from the pain.
Pacifying the hurt,
Numbing your heart in its despair.
The struggle to ignore the obvious
Collapsing of your soul can be monumental.
The trauma of your existence
Can be too much to bear,
Too much to endure.
Yet the pain you go through will heal you.
For in the midst of complete and true
Hopelessness,
Lies the antidote for your release.

Purging

As I reach inside myself
I see so much I hate
I'm a conflict of my own interest.

I grab deep inside of me
 all the anger, jealousy, hatred,

And as I rip it out of me,
I bleed out all my emotions, in pain.

I scream out all of the sadness I've bottled up for far too long.
As I see the dark black hole inside of me,
I finally start to see room for something good to grow

To start a fire that has never burned before.
To start anew…
And, I start to heal.

My Dear Husband...

How do I begin...
To tell you that my heart does not beat without you.
How do I begin to tell you that the air I breath is sweet in taste
because of the memories we share.
Painful also is the past mistakes you and I have together.
The error of our ways have made defined lines in our eyes
from our grief and to face the sadness we have because of them.
We both see each other through glasses that are beveled.
Seeing the profound impacts that are enhanced
while the true definition of our life together is asked by the side.
I cannot see my hand without your hand next to it,
nor can I wake up the next day and not see the handsome man
that shares my bed every day.
You are intertwined in my heart like the veins that are sewn into
my heart,
to keep my blood flowing constantly.
You are a part of me always.
You hold my life, my spirit, my heart.
Always.

My Daughter

My daughter came along
 On a spring day,
When the world was in chaos
And full of dismay.
She was a surprise to us both you see.
Because doctors said she could not be.
But against all odds she found a way
And came to us in the month of May
We had a chance to have our own
Bundle of joy, and bring her home.

My Son

My son brought me a flower today.
It's sweet aroma,
the beautiful mountain laurel.
My memories as a child,
they rush inside my head.
The sweet memories
Of climbing those beautiful branches.
Oh, the fragrance of the Laurel!
My son brought me a flower today
 and it's sprung forth Sweetness in my heart.
For on the edge of wanting death,
he brought me back to life.

Last Moments

Cold air all around me and I choose to breathe it in.
 It fills my lungs with winter.
 As I slowly exhale, I feel my sadness engulfing me.
I'm surrounded by the quite presence of Autumn.
As it starts to bid farewell, Winter takes its place.
The bird's songs are a distant memory
 as the rustling of leaves fill the air.
 They fall to the ground as they elegantly die.
 I see their true colors as they lay,
 it's last moment to shine in hues of red, orange and brown.
No birds on branches, no leaves on branches,
just branches lonely with one another.
All is quiet, no wind, no songs.
 I start to look in anticipation of the spring when all things wake up.
So, until then I will sit here in silence, in hope,
that like the spring, my heart will awaken again.

Rest my Heart

Rest my heart upon your hands
And give my mind some peace
Take my voice that sings so sad
And give my soul release.

The light that glows like embers
Have all the sudden gone out
Inside here it's always December
Where nothing will dare sprout.

I'm Sorry

On the edge of my own extinction
I grab onto my heart and say:
I'm sorry I didn't keep you from
Feeling so much pain.
I'm sorry I didn't hold you
And keep you from the rain.
I wish I could have given you
Peace ,and calm within.
Instead, I ignored you constantly
While you beat under my skin.
I'm sorry I didn't consider you
For moments when I was in doubt.
I should have turned to you quickly
But I was completely tuned out.
I should have fed you love
Instead of loneliness and dread.
But now I must be on my way
Because without you...I'm dead.

This Moment

In this moment of stagnation,
I hold my breath and realize
that soon I'll come back to life
and start to breathe again.

Determined

Let's go to the beginning
Where everything was quiet
Where everything was simple
Where everything was warm
You weren't sure of the world
But you did know one thing:
You were safe.

Now everything is crazy
And everything is loud
Nothing is as it seems
And you feel lost
You have lost hope
And maybe some faith
But someday, this will pass
And you will have strength

So don't let go
Keep moving forward
The best is yet to come
Because you will have grown
You will be wiser
And you will gain courage
You will defeat
So go out and fight!

Control

To quiet my mind
To block out all noise
It's so difficult to do this
So difficult indeed.
The rambling and noises
That are constant and flowing
Are difficult to control
When I lose control.
I try to think of smiles, and laughter, I do.
In hopes it will bring me back.
I long for the night when nothing is asked of me.
For then I can think of nothing ,but what I love.

Water

Oh please, let me be washed clean and be made new!
Let the water wash off the dirt of my sins.
Let the water clean off the oil of my deceptions and jealousy I have left behind.
Let the old flakes of my lies and anger flow off with the water
And see it all fall into the sea of forgiveness.
Please let me vomit out all my hate and resentment
So that my stomach can settle and be at peace.

Cut me, please, on my arm
And let the blood that is carried through my heart and my whole body
Empty out all the resentment and wickedness I have ever felt for anyone or anything
So, then my heart can once again beat strong and good.
My wound will heal over, and my heart will be at peace.

Tests

Sometimes our biggest tests are the smallest things we face daily.
We know we are worth more, but no one cares.
We think of others, but they don't think of us.
We fight for our sanity
While others want us to break.
We work hard for what we have, while some want us to lose it all.
Life is not about our failures, our losses, or our disappointments. It's about what we've learned—that we tried—that we stood in that arena and gave it all we had! Our test is whether or not we have what it takes to stay in the game.
 Win or lose, hold on and stay!!!

Conquer

My quill quakes in fury
As my heart is trembling in fear
My past has come back to torment me
Yet I will not shed a tear

My coiled hair is tied back
My sleeves are pulled up
I sit and steadily wait for the attack
My coffee hot in the cup.

Wanting to give in
And succumb to my pain
But wanting so much to win
My feelings I do contain.

On the Verge

Some of us are lost,
Trying to find our way.
We are torn at heart and mind.
We are divided.
Seeking the truth and
Taking deep breaths
So, we don't die from the starvation of our soul.
On the verge of complete insanity,
We close our eyes in hopes that
We won't delve into despair.
No time for tears,
No time for second guessing.
We must move forward,
To catch what we have lost.
To mend our moment in time
And, finally, be able to live again.

Bracing

I came upon a moment one day
When all was going right
When something came from out of the blue
And forced me to stop and fight
I had to throw down all I had and got ready for the pain
I had to brace myself and remember,
There was going to be some rain.
Some thunder started and some lighting.
I knew what was coming next.
My heart was beating fast as
 I felt it burst out of my chest.
The devastation was real
It was disastrous to the soul
Things wouldn't be the same
Since I had little or no control.
I want to run and hide
To escape this time in hell
To go back to times of happiness
To go back to peace as well.

The Battle

Don't fall into temptation,
For you will only find
Failure and frustration
And loss of peace of mind

Your life will be a debacle
A total loss, in fact
You won't even be able to tackle
Your life, so you must act.

You must be so courageous
Even in the midst of pain
Your strength will be your advantage
To battle in the rain

Your power will be from above
As he grants you all you need
To defeat all evil with love
And to be valiant, to be free!

Hope

I will not step in to the darkness of my mind
Where the feelings of despair and loneliness are running constantly.
Where shattered pasts and darker futures wait to be unlocked.
I have felt the cold of unwanted love,
And the abandonment of those who were supposed to love me.
I have crawled the floors of sadness to see a glimpse of hope.
There is light that creeps between the shadows on the floor.
It's difficult to reach as the darkness want to hold me captive for days even months.
I will hold on to my light until the flame goes out.
I will hold it dear to me, while I search of ways to keep it lit.

Inner child

As the inner child awakens,
Her eyes see blurry.
She stretches and succumbs to pain.
The tears of past trauma,
Tears of lost moments,
Never to get back.
Tossing in pain from the struggles
To breath, to live, to adapt.
Walking to the mirror,
She sees her hair unbrushed.
Neglect has made its nest there.
Face is dirty, from unwanted words.
Words full of pain
Wanting to start the day new,
But needing to work through
It all. The worst of it all.
And as she starts to deal, and cry
She starts to heal, and fly
As her spirit starts to emerge
She sees hope..
She sees tomorrow.

The Contract

The terms and conditions that were laid out before me
 as I was brought into this world,
 Would not have been those that
 Would have been signed and approved
  Of by me.
  And yet here I am living by those terms and conditions.
  I've learned to accept the good and the bad
The best and the worst.
With these terms I've learned to adapt and work with the limitations I've been given.
And even though these terms were as followed
 And have been followed,
 I've allowed myself not to be defined by them.
 I will only define myself by myself worth and determination to go on.
 And fight for what is right,
 To stand by my family,
 And face the awful world with hope.
 So that one day,
 When my contract is finished,
 They will say to all, "She did it all, She faced it all"
With strength and hope
And love most of all.

The Path

Emerging from the darkness
Of my soul…
So, trickles forth
Assurance and foresight…
This I know to be true
I will grow stronger…
Wiser—and confident
In myself…
The future has no map of where to go
I must give it direction…
So, I will follow the path that leads to my salvation—
The path that will lead me to my happiness…
The path that will lead me home
I have many roads before me…
But with confidence in myself
I will choose the right path
The bright path…
And leave my darkness behind me.

A Moment in Time

A moment in time
> To feel calm ,
> To feel ease

A moment in time
> To think of what was
> And what can be.

A moment to reflect
> To ponder and to see
>> That such a quiet moment
>> Can be quick and free

A moment so rare
> Is often so in need
>> To have it, is priceless
>>> To have it, indeed.

Thankful

I thank God each day
That I'm alive, and so I pray.
I pray for the beautiful night
And the stars that shine so bright
For the love he has shown to me
And the creations we can see
I pray that I might live forever
To be in Paradise eternal.
I pray for all bad thoughts to go
So that I might see his love grow.
I thank him for the little things
I seem to take for certainty—
Things I will never take for granted
Like the opportunity I've been handed
To love and to forgive
To be patient and to live
I love my God and my family
And my life for all eternity.

Rise

Give me your hand
And show me your bravery
Your dynamic posture in the midst of pain
You Leave me beside myself in awe
It's your constant progress and resolve
To rise above it all
Great or small
To show your brilliance and strength.

One day

One day the birds will sing,
For there will be great peace.
They will fly above the clouds,
For they have been released.

The sun will be bursting through
A clear and bright blue sky
Showing all its glory
Every time you go outside

Your day will start out fresh
As your body will feel brand new
And your work with your own hands,
Will be what you WANT to do.

The house you will build to live in
Will be all your dreams come true
The rooms will be filled with laughter
And your faith will be renewed

So, press on through this life that breaks us
And be brave through every day,
For soon YOU will be released.
This world is not far away.

"May you always
Rise from your fall
Seek peace in chaos
Heal from your wounds
Be victorious in loss"

-Monica C. Crum

A Note about my Family

As it turned out... Beelzebub had a devil for a son... and a daughter

It's a hard grasp at which straw was the one that broke the camel's back, but there is one thing for sure—the camel never had a chance. Chicken or the egg. Chicken. Eggs. Let's hash out the base ingredients.

Mother... we will call her an egg donor. She had her fair share of emotional, physical, and sexual abuse as a child. As my brother once said, "Through my umbilical cord, she pumped her emotional waste into [us]."

Dad was raised in a divided house. (Grandpa remarried and had another family).

Grandma never remarried, and her Roman Catholic house provided the much-needed reason for my grandfather to stay gone.

A 1950s baby boomer, my father spent his early years as an altar boy working his way up the parochial ranks. With no father figure but the one in a robe at church, he told stories of angry nuns smacking his hands with the yardstick. According to him, those were the highlights of his rearing—that, and Grandma throwing shoes around corners. (So, the story goes.)

The way I see it, his views regarding fatherhood were bent and warped into a fashion where only a narcissist can breed. And that is how you spell disaster!

Then, when he became an adult, he had a shotgun wedding in a racially charged household, so it was never going to end right.

Grandma only let it happen because there were going to be two of us. That date— June 1st, 1973—is a day in the calendar that can only be surmised as National Narcissistic Survivorship Day.

My brother wanted to tell his story. He wanted to air it all out—purge the demons and shout it to the world. He never got that chance. He only wrote the introduction, a dedication to our grandmother. I couldn't write this book without including it—without including him.

Eddie's Introduction

At the age of eight, I had already come to the realization that it was me versus my family in a way that no child should ever have to endure. With torture executed on a daily basis, I was ready to die, but before that was to happen, the decision to bring the rest of my family with me was something I struggled with on a daily basis until my 14th birthday.

It was 1987 when the only friend and lifesaver in my life passed away, and with her, she took all hope of ever living through the horrific childhood I was experiencing. The day Grandma died, I died—and the chance of ever having a normal life was gone forever.

A long, dark night sat on my heart, and for the next 27 years, I would dwell in the asylum of my mind, battling regret, anger, hatred—and the demons that no one dares to talk about. Since I am writing this from a free view of the street and not through bars, I obviously won that battle and the rest that followed. But to the victor doesn't always go to spoils.

This story you are about to hear is real, and the thoughts I have decided to release to share my ordeal with domestic violence as a child are a little graphic and very personal. You see, we have become a people that would rather watch a movie about the elephant in the room than discuss it.

Well, I'm about to bring many elephants into the room. I hope there's room for us all. This is dedicated to my grandmother, who lives in Paradise already. The thought of her being disappointed in any action that I might have taken against my family has kept me minding her long after her death, and to this day, I still long for her hugs and kisses.

"I love you, Grandma! I'll see you in Paradise soon. You don't wait up for me. I'll be there eventually!"

Epilogue

My poetry details my experiences and acuity throughout my life, though my perception is fluid, and perhaps that's because mental illness has shaped my world. I inherited bipolar disorder from my mother. Throw in abuse, and you have an awful storm brewing. If I hadn't endured abuse, conceivably, my life would have been better.

Mental illness is nothing to joke around about. It's a serious issue that affects over 52.9 million people in the US, as noted in 2020. Some people with mental illness actually go to a doctor to seek help, but millions more are too afraid or just don't think it's important enough to take care of themselves. So many people struggle every day just to open their eyes and breathe.

I sought help in my thirties. I had been struggling with issues of depression and suicidal thoughts since I was six. That's a long time to go without help.

Therapy has helped me. It showed me that it's not my fault that I was abused. It also taught me techniques to change my way of thinking, and it has encouraged me to reassure myself that it's up to me to shape my future.

I won't let my illness take over me! Neither should you. Some of you may not suffer from mental issues, but you may know someone battling with this. Please stress to them that they are important, and encourage them to get help.

If we all help each other, the rewards are great!

Acknowledgements

Thanks to..

My husband. You have done your best to support me through all these years. I can't thank you enough for always being my voice of reason. For being my rock. Thank you for listening to all my poems. Thank you for everything. I love you .

My children. My goodness, where would I be without you all? I dreamed of you all, but never knew how deep my love would go. You have taught me so many lessons. But most of all, to enjoy the little things. I love you all so much. To the moon and back.

To my Aunt Mima. You have been there from the beginning. Thank you for being there from my early years, to graduation, to my children's births, to my brother's death. And all the years in-between. You gave me so much strength at times when I had none. I love you.

Thank you to Kimberly my editor. For giving me the chance to show you my poetry. I know it wasn't a big genre to write in, but you gave me your time and energy and expertise, and I appreciate it all. I can't thank you enough.

Thank you Blair for giving me that break I needed. You have been a blessing .

And last but not least,

Harry. Thank you for inviting us to your house for some grape juice, and introducing me to Matilda. What a wonderful day we had.

About the Author

Monica C. Crum

Monica is a San Antonio-based poet, child development expert, and engineer, who has been writing since the age of 12. With a decade of experience teaching preschool and a profound personal journey marked by mental health struggles, Monica's poetry is deeply informed by her experiences. Her collection, *"Nena No More,"* confronts the shadows of depression, self-harm, and abuse, while also reflecting on the loss of her twin brother. Despite these challenges, Monica's writing has been a sanctuary, offering solace and hope. A passionate advocate for children and a dedicated mother of three, Monica finds joy in family, fishing, and autumn's beauty. Her work aims to illuminate the path for those navigating similar darkness, affirming that even amid despair, hope persists.

www.ingramcontent.com/pod-product-compliance
Lightning Source LLC
LaVergne TN
LVHW092051060526
838201LV00047B/1344